A Little Peace of Me

A Little Peace of Me
Deborah F. Hayes

3Seats Publishing
2020

Silence

This Realistic fiction is a genre consisting of stories and poetry that could have occurred to people or animals in a believable setting. These stories and poetry resemble real life, and fictional characters within these stories react similarly to real people. Readers expect Fiction to reflect the real world; they do not expect it to portray the real world.

Copyright © 2019 A Little Peace of Me by Deborah F. Hayes.

All rights reserved. No part of this publication may be reproduced, distributed, or transmitted in any form or by any means, including photocopying, recording, or other electronic or mechanical methods, without the prior written permission of the publisher, except in the case of brief quotations embodied in critical reviews and certain other noncommercial uses permitted by copyright law. For permission requests, write to the Publisher, addressed "Attention: Permissions Coordinator," at the address below.

3Seats Publishing
Virginia Beach, Virginia
3Seatspublishing@gmail.com

Cover Illustration by Stanley Barros Liete
Cover and Book Design by 3Seats Publishing
Editing by 3Seats Publishing

ISBN 13:-978-0-9986303-5-9
ISBN # for eBook: pending
Library of Congress Control Number: 2020903818

First Edition May 2020
Printed in the USA by Lulu, Inc. of Raleigh, NC 27607

Calmness

Dedication

This book is dedicated to my father in the gospel, late **Bishop Andrew C. Jackson**. Many years ago, Bishop Jackson heard a poem I had written and recited at a Sunday afternoon Church Service. He said, "Debbie" {as he used to call me}, you need to write that poem down and put it in a book of Poetry".

Well Bishop, many years later and after many times of picking up the pen and putting it down again, here it is. Thank You, Bishop Jackson, for those words of Inspiration they remain with me until this day.

Finally, this book is also dedicated to the memory of my sweet angel, **Mag**. Mom you gave me life and even though you're no longer here you still live inside of me.

I'll Love You Always,

Deborah

Contents

~~ Acknowledgments

~~ Preface

~ To My Young Single Mothers on 'Mother's Day' ~ 1
~ What Happens after Christmas? ~ 2
~ Magnolia ~ 3
~ A Man of GOD ~ 4
~ Slothfulness ~ 5
~ The Good News Is: God is Bigger than That ~ 6
~ Creator, Provider ~ 7
~ I Couldn't TELL THEM ~ 8 & 9
~ Shh… ~ 10
~ Act like a Woman; Think like GOD! ~ 11
~ He Is, We Are, And He Was! ~ 12
~ Prepared and Ready ~ 13
~ The Pit ~ 14
~ It takes Work, to do what's Right! ~ 15
~ For Us, You Were Crucified ~ 16
~ Charge to the Deacons and Wives ~ 17
~ Dear God ~ 18 &19
~ A Slice of Bacon, Is It Worth It? ~ 20
~ Are We Ever Satisfied, Everyday Can't Be Friday ~ 21
~ That's What You Get for Being Late on 1st Sunday ~ 22
~ Where Does My Passion, Lie? ~ 23
~ A Covering ~ 24
~ Complete ~ 25
~ Baby Girl ~ 26
~ I USED THE DISHWASHER TODAY ~ 27
~ Everything You Need, GOD's got it! ~ 28
~ I Saw a Little Bird Sitting on a Tree ~ 29
~ I Give You My Permission ~ 30
~ Still Alive ~ 31
~ What a Week! ~ 32
~ Salt ~ 33
~ Committed? ~ 34
~~ Notes ~ 35

Peace

Quiet

Serenity

Acknowledgments

To my friend M. Martin who gave me a pen and pencil set several Christmases ago to help me get started on this project; to L. Dixon my friend, my beautician and my exercise guru, thank you for providing me with a comfort journal during the passing of my mother. From this journal, I entered my daily thoughts that are now being published in this book.

To my niece S. Dwight, who encourages me more than, you know. I am so Proud of You. And to my GNO's, thanks for encouraging me to keep my vision.

To my sister Lynetta, the best secretary, my counselor and my earthly angel. Even to this day she still looks out for and takes care of me. Ill love you forever.

And to my cousin...Owner and President of 3Seats publishing. Thank you for believing in me.

Yes, it may only be a few pages but from these pages I give you,
A Little Peace of Me

Tranquility

Preface

As I stated in my dedication, my father in the gospel the late Bishop A.C. Jackson heard me read a poem at an afternoon church program many, many years ago. He told me to write it down and put it in a book. Do I remember what the poem was, no, but because Bishop said it, that's just what you did.

Timing of the book- As you begin to read through these pages, you will find different timelines in my writings. A few of them are recent but the majority are from many years before. Some came in moments, some in days and some through the years in different settings and seasons. God and his peace were there during many settings. Many while I was riding in my car on my way to work.

Many of the things I wrote about I saw happening around me. I knew of people who suffered from domestic violence. I saw a friend's marriage break up after several years.

GOD often spoke to me in quiet times, like sitting on the porch in the hills of the mountains listening to the rain, or on the balcony of a beach hotel being calmed by the waves flowing from the ocean.

Harmony

To My Young, Single Mother's on 'Mother's Day'

As Mother's Day approaches, yes, we will celebrate the mothers and
Seniors of old!
But on this day, I'll honor you because you're Young,
Courageous and Bold!
I thought about you as I drove into work;
Your faces came to my mind.
Although I don't know all of your names;
The vision that God gave was surely right on time.

You're the one who drives the kids to school each and every day,
The one, who volunteers, comes to every meeting,
School play and a member of the PTA.
I see you as you bring your son(s) and daughter(s) to church;
While sometimes they sit beside you,
Other times they want to walk away and lurch.

I also see you working in different ministries;
Helping, greeting and serving those who are also in need;
Encouraging them in their growth, to prosper and succeed.

So keep bringing your children to church and continue
To pray for them as we know we should.
Someday they will see that it worked together for their good.

Your friend Deborah, been there, done that

What Happens after Christmas?

The tree has now been put away; the toys are nowhere to be found,
No more dinner parties and the lights have been taken down:

Did you get your heart's desires from everything on your list?
Or are you pouting because some items had been missed?
Are you now walking the tread and doing pushups on the floor
Or are you running to the gym and is the first one at the door?

There are a few strings of tinsel still glistening here and there.
Our memories still fresh in your mind, and will they always be there?
Has the immediate family gone back to their respective homes?
Some in the mountains, in the cities and some where the buffalo roam.

Now it is after Christmas and all has settled down
The kids are back in school, some smiling some with a frown
Santa's gone back to the North Pole preparing for next year
But will it take us that long to spread everyday cheer?

What about the homeless man lying on the street:
Will you still go out every Saturday and give him food to eat?
What about the mom living in the shelter with her 4 kids
Will we visit them before next Christmas or will our faces be hidden?

Don't forget those Stockings that we filled at the job;
So those who have nothing will not begin to rob,
Oh yeah, and the bells we rang
And some dropped money in the kettle
Are we now sitting back, our heart's content and feeling all settled?

Let us not forget the gifts and the joy that we shared at Christmas time.
It may have been a few days for us, but for some, it is a lifetime.

Magnolia

Her mother named her Magnolia because she is as
Sweet and Strong as the flower itself.
When she leaves a room her fragrance still remains.
The atmosphere states that she has blessed us with her presence.
Her leaves remain green because
She stays rooted and grounded in the word of God.
The tears she sheds in her private time allow God to
Prune her for better times to come.

If anyone finds fault in her
It's only because they envy the spirit that lives inside of her.
She never once complained but through it all,
She gave God all the Glory.

Extravagant things she did not always have
Because the Gift of God was more precious to her
Than material things could ever be.

Oh, how she could stir up a time of devotion and praise.
She loved to sing, 'There is room at the Cross for me'.
She has found her place at the cross and can now
Stand boldly before the Throne.
As God, I know, has welcomed her into his Kingdom.

Yes, she was a precious flower and yet her fragrance still remains.

Our Mother, grandmother, sister and our friend, Mrs. Magnolia Francis.
Mom- Laid to rest 4/13/2009. Ten years have come and gone so fast,
There were many days I thought I wouldn't last.
Yes, hurt and sorrow still come now and then;
But joy takes over because I know I'll see you again.

A Man of GOD

This poem is dedicated to my husband William.

There are days when I haven't done the best that I can do,
Because my ultimate goal Lord is to please you.
This year certain things happened that I did not expect;
Some I had to hold on to and some I had to reject.

You gave me a space of quiet time, to heal my body I thought;
But in that precious quiet time my undivided attention you caught.
You made me realize I am but a man
And that all things come from you,
And with the grip of your powerful hand,
You pulled me and my family through.

You know I love my family they mean the world to me,
I try to do what's best for them but sometimes they don't see.
They don't always see my sacrifice as a husband and a dad,
I try to share with them what you've given me
But when they don't listen I get a little sad.

I want them to be thankful for the things you've blessed us with;
So that when you're ready we'll be prepared
To receive even greater gifts.

They presented me with a plaque last night,
One I don't think I deserved.
I could have done a better job, in my time to serve.
No, I didn't attend every service or visit all the sick or made every call;
But I thank you, Dear Lord, for blessing me
And for seeing me through it all.

Slothfulness

During November and December, our Sunday School Class has been discussing the seven deadly sins. Each student had to pick one of the sins and discuss how it related to their lives or how it affected them. Sad to say, I picked slothfulness. How does this relate to me? Well, today is December 31st the last day in the year of 2011 and I'm just putting the final words in this project/request that was given to me over ten years ago. Was this the appointed time to complete this mission or was this another act of slothfulness? You'll see or I'll tell you within the next few months?

Yes, I would have to call it slothfulness, because it's been another eight years since I wrote the last statement.

Lord, please let this project still be a gift you have given to me and not just something of myself. Continue to work on me in my state of overcoming Slothfulness. Amen

The Good News Is: God is Bigger than That

Sickness~
Bad news from the doctor: ~ The Good News Is: God is Bigger than That ~ By His stripes we are Healed. I'm blessed by what one of the Mother's on the prayer Line said the other day. "...her hearing may be lost in one ear... but then she said she can always get a hearing aid"...that's good news!

Laid Off~
After 25 years of dedication they tell you they don't need your services anymore: ~ The Good News Is: God is Bigger than That. ~
He said I will supply all of your needs according to his riches in glory by Christ Jesus.

Marital Problems~
When your husband or wife starts acting up or tipping and dipping: ~ The Good News Is: God is Bigger than That. ~
He said all things work together for the Good of them who Love God and who are the Called according to His purpose.

Financial Problems~
The Good News Is: God is Bigger than That. ~
He said to bring all your tithes and offerings into the storehouse and there will be Meat in his house.

Children Problems~
Acting up in school, disobedience, ~ The Good News Is: God is Bigger than That. ~ He said train up a child in the way that he should go and when he is old he will not depart from it.

Identity Crisis~
The Good News Is: God is Bigger than That. ~ God created man in his image.

Death~
The Good News Is: He conquered death, hell, and the grave! For those of us who die in Christ we are still victorious, why, because:
God Is Bigger than That.

Creator, Provider

My Heavenly Father, you made the Heavens and the Earth
The sun to light the sky by day,
And the moon and the stars in the sky by night
You made every living thing and you made each one of us...
You said your work was good.
So, I pray I am in a position to know
You have provided everything I need...
Even through your death on the cross
You've given me what I need to receive salvation
And to preach the gospel to those whom I may encounter.

Lord, thank you for letting me know that
My healing and deliverance are already done in Jesus' name, Amen.

I Couldn't TELL THEM!
{Before we came to church this morning}

When I walked into the church this morning everyone told me how pretty I looked. They told me my smile lit up the whole place...I couldn't tell them that the smile on my face was not for real, it was just hiding the pain that was inside my heart.

They said my make-up looked really good and my face was glowing. I told them, thank you. I couldn't tell them that the makeup was hiding the black-eye he gave me ~ before we came to church this morning.

They saw me limping just a little and asked what happened. I told them I tripped over something that was on the floor. I couldn't tell them that what I tripped over was his leg that he deliberately stuck out as I walked by so I could fall down ~ before we came to church this morning.

They said they saw me on the monitor screen worshiping my God and praising Him with tears in my eyes. I couldn't tell them the tears they saw were not tears of worship but I was crying because while we were in the car he told me I am nothing, never was nothing and never would be nothing ~ before we came to church this morning.

Oh, but look at him now, greeting the members, reading the scripture, saying the prayer and even helping with the morning offering. Smiling and saying 'Praise the Lord' to everyone. Then he welcomes the visitors saying, "I and my beautiful wife (doesn't she look lovely today) along with the members of the congregation want to thank you for joining us today!

Continued...

I told her how beautiful she looked ~ before we came to church this morning". Then he winks at me with a smile and a smirk, the congregation responded with oohs and aahs, but I know that wink means if I tell anybody anything about what's been going on before we came to church this morning, I know what will be waiting for me when I get home.

The Sister...who sits next to me on the front row says, "You are so blessed to have a wonderful man of God like that in your life. Someone who loves you and treats you like a queen and you look so good together, yes, the perfect couple". And then she says, maybe one-day God will send me a man just like that. My tears start to flow again...*because I couldn't tell them.*

My Prayer,
Dear Lord my Heavenly Father, I'm at a crossroads in my life. Lord I know I hold a big position in the church, I know others look up to me, I know my name is well known in the neighborhood and community. But Lord, I also know that you have not given me the spirit of fear but of power and a sound mind. Lord, I know people will talk, those at the church will be hurt. But Lord I can't go through this anymore, 15 years is too long and long enough. Lord, I've been silent too long, but even through this, others will know that you are a deliverer and a keeper.
And I Thank You, Amen....

Oh yes and one more thing...hello, 911. My name is Mrs. Church Lady... and I'd like to report...that my husband, Rev. Preacher... yes, that's the one down at Mt Baptist AME Church...has been abusing me for over 15 years and I'm tired of it. Yes...him. Yes...him. Where can you find him...well, let me tell you......

Shh…

Shh… If I cook the dinner just right tonight, maybe he won't get mad and throw the food on the floor this time and if I clean the house really good, maybe he won't yell so loud when he gets home.

Shh… If I keep the children quiet and don't talk so loud, maybe he'll be in a good mood.

Shh… He said he loved me and he wouldn't do it again. And since we're engaged, I know he'll change when we get married.

Shh… Just because he calls me out my name and curses at me I know I can change him, if I just hang on a little while longer.

Shh… He said he wants me to keep my cell phone with me so he'll know where I am at all times because he loves me. Even though he hits me sometimes, I still have to stay with him because he pays all the bills.

Shh… He said he had a bad day and didn't mean to hit me so hard, this time.

Shh… I can't leave because I and my children have no place to go. And he said if I left he would hunt me down and kill me.

Shh… If I bring home good grades, maybe mommy & daddy won't be mean to me and hit me this time.

Shh… Yes, I'm a teacher and that little boy is my student and yes, I saw the bruises on his little back several times, but I thought he was just playing with his school mates.

Shh… Yes, she's my best friend and told me she wanted to talk, but I was busy that day.

Shh… Yes, I saw him push her, a couple of times when they thought I wasn't looking, but I didn't want to interfere.

Shh… Why are we whispering? Because we're in the funeral procession. Who's funeral? My best friend, that student, that woman, that man, that executive, that teacher, that preacher, that wife, that husband, that neighbor…

What happened? Shhhhhhhh.

Act like a Woman; Think like God!

I'm told to **act like a woman and think like God** when my husband just told me he doesn't love me anymore. He said after 15 years he was tired of being married and wanted to go and find out what he had been missing. I'm told to act like a woman and think like God... When we made a promise 'until death do we part'.

What about the children?" I asked, he said, "Well I never really wanted to be a father anyway you can raise them"... How? I said. You promised that you would take care of me and the children. You said you wanted me to stay home and take care of the house and the family. I did all that, I cleaned the house, I cooked your breakfast every morning and I had your dinner prepared every night. I dusted, I mopped, I did the carpool with the children, I took your clothes to the cleaners and picked them up, I said **yes** on many nights when I wanted to say no... I planned birthday parties and all of your office parties and I balanced the checkbooks. What about money for me and the kids- "Speaking of money", he said, "I've taken all the bank accounts out of our names and put them only in my name." How are we supposed to live and get by I asked- "the best way you can, he said, get a job." I had a job before we got married but you told me I didn't have to work, now I have no skills, I haven't worked in over 20 years. "Oh well", he said and he was gone. And I'm to act like a woman and think like God?

Romans 8:35-39
The trouble and hardships that I'm facing now "I won't let this separate me from the love of Christ? Yes, like a sheep, I've been slaughtered." Even in all these things, I am more than a conqueror through Christ who does love me. Yes, he may have taken the money and closed all of the bank accounts in my name but I know my God shall supply all of my needs according to His riches in Glory by Christ Jesus. And His riches are so much more. I'm going to cast all my cares upon God; for I'm confident in knowing that He cares for me and that He will never leave me or forsake me.

What did I say about those skills I have? Planning parties at the school, the office is organized, balancing our bank accounts for all those years...Event Planning, me? Back to School me? *HE said my daughter, you're going to take this pain and turn it into something great!*

He Is, We Are, And He Was!

We've been married for 30 years. He is my first love ever since high school. He is my best friend, my lover, my confidant. We laugh, we talk, we cry, we pray, we encourage each other. He finishes my sentences before I'm even through talking. He sends me flowers just because... I make his favorite dessert every now and then just because... He calls me in the middle of the day just to see how I am doing? Sometimes I surprise him at the office and take him out to lunch. We've raised the children, now their grown and have families of their own. I'm so excited... we're getting ready for our vacation, just the two of us... some well-deserved getaway time. The bags are packed, passports, cash, and camera ready... everyone has been contacted, the mail will be picked up...yes... We are ready.

He should have been back from the store by now...hmm. He's been gone for a very long time. I hope he's ok. I think I'll call him on his cell phone...hmm, no answer. I'll try again in a few minutes... hmm ok, still no answer. Another hour went by! Still no word. Hmm...! Maybe he saw an old friend and started talking or stopped by his brother's house... I'll call over there.

Oh, you haven't talked with him today... I'm worried now. Oh, that's the doorbell he must have forgotten his keys... I open the door, that's not him... why are there 2 policemen at my door...? Why do they look so sad...? `Excuse me, Ma'am, Are you Mrs. ...' Yes, I am. 'Is your husband's name Mr. ...?' Yes it is. `May we come in? There was an accident on the highway and we're sorry to have to tell you this but..........'

We were married for over 30 years... He was my first love... he was my best friend... he was... he was... he was... My husband of over 30 years is suddenly gone. Why God, Why? I'm hurt, I'm angry ...why God, Why?

John 14:27 *"Peace I leave with you, my peace I give unto you: not as the world giveth, give I unto you. Let not your heart be troubled, neither let it be afraid." (KJV)*

Isaiah 41:10-13 *"... I will strengthen thee; yea, I will help thee; yea, I will uphold thee with the right hand of my righteousness... For I the LORD thy God will hold thy right hand, saying unto thee, Fear not; I will help thee." (KJV)*

Prepared and Ready

I hear some folks say that when women reach a certain age,
They probably won't be able to find a suitable mate for marriage.
Or they may not be able to take care of themselves.
Well, let me tell you what a Godly woman, who thinks like God,
Can accomplish.

God has already prepared me to be what he wants me to be.
He's provided for me to complete my
Master's Degree in Financial Accounting.
I'm the head of my own business and have several employees,
Who reports to me, yes, even some men.

My house will be paid for in the next 2 years
And my new car is ready to be picked up.
I'm a good cook, (thanks mom), I handle my finances very well,
I am a good housekeeper if I say so myself.
I'm a reader and student of His Word;
I live a Godly, healthy and pure life,
And I carry myself in a manner that is pleasing to my God.

The day I accepted Christ, He became the head of my life
And he directs me in the way that I should go.
He said he would provide me with any and everything I need.
When I get lonely and certain thoughts enter my mind,
He directs me to his word and lets me know he is my comforter.

So, if God's will for me is to marry,
I don't have to go looking for Mr...., he'll find me.
He'll know that everything he desires in a wife is
Already in place prepared and ready.
And if God wants me to remain committed to him,
I'm in place, prepared and I'm ready.

The Pit

I found myself standing in the middle of a pit
And wondered how I got there.
That very thing that used to bring me joy,
I have allowed it to bring sorrow to my soul.
I've allowed it to consume me with darkness.
That very thing I used to boast and brag about,
I now have to pump myself up even when I begin to speak about it
Sometimes forcing it with a smile.
With this thing, I am weak in my own strength,
So I have to call on God to renew my strength through His joy.
Did I get here on my own; did God place me here? I don't know!
Even though it may seem a little dark right now,
I did notice that the top of this pit is not covered.
There's still an opening for the sunlight to come through.
There still is a way for me to escape!

It takes Work, to do what's Right!

It takes Work, to do what's right.
Sometimes you have to try with all your might.
To do well in school you have to study hard.
Sometimes you may have to miss playing in the schoolyard.

It takes Work, to do what's right.
When others are gossiping, your mouth you must keep tight.
When exercising the body, you can't eat heavy
You have to eat light.

It takes Work, to do what's right.
When Satan says go ahead,
It's only for one night.
Don't forget, {one night} can affect the rest of your life.

It takes Work, to do what's right.
When you see money fall to the floor
And you know it does not belong to you,
You must find to whom it belongs,
Because it's the right thing to do.

It takes Work, to do what's right.
When your eyes start to wonder on that lady or that man
Who is not your husband or wife.
You must remember you made a vow
That you must keep for the rest of your life.

It takes Work, to do what's right.
It may be easier just to do things that are wrong.
You can say, nobody sees, nobody cares
But please keep in mind, that the
{Right}eous one is always watching and is always there!

For Us, You Were Crucified

We were bought with a price no man can repay.
As they hung you on the cross and your body did lay.

They twisted a crown of thorns and placed it on your head;
They spit, mocked and beat you just because they wanted you dead.
~ No Sin you committed, no harm you had done,
Would anyone else pay this price? No not one.

The cross laid high and it laid tall,
For this great sacrifice, you made
~ not just for one but you made it for all.
For all, of us have sinned and fallen short of your word,
But you spoke with Your Father He listened and He heard.

You said, 'Father forgive them, for they know not what they do'
~ Not just the ones that day at the cross ~
But He also pleaded for me and He pleaded for you.

For Us, You Were Crucified; for the way, we sometimes walk,
The ungodly things we do and often by the way we talk.
We speak with such doubt and we live with such fear,
Knowing You've Told Us You Would Always Be Near.

We must now plead the blood that ran down from your hand,
Because One Day before You We All Must Stand.

Charge to the Deacons and Wives

We've fellowshipped together behind these closed doors,
Thanking God for the blessings we've received in 2004.
But as we walk outside these doors,
That's when the task begins,
To help those who are lost run away from sin.

God has given us a purpose
And a calling on our lives,
To be Peaceable to all men
And to refrain from causing strife.

Yes, we are only humans
But we are also saints,
Knowing that through Christ we can
And without Him, we can't.

Deacons love your wives as God so loved the church;
Continue to do your duties;
But please don't forget about her.

So, as we leave to go back to our normal daily lives,
Don't forget and always remember
That our # 1 business is still
To win souls for Christ.

Dear God

Dear God,
My best friend is hurting. She sees the man she fell in love with turning into someone she doesn't even know. Her home is not at peace. What shall I tell my friend? ~Deb
God ~ Tell her, that all things are working together for the good!

Dear God,
My best friend is at a difficult point in her life and doesn't know which way to turn. What shall I tell her? ~Deb
God ~ Tell her, to trust in me with all her heart and lean not to her Own understanding and in all her ways acknowledge me and I will direct her path.

Dear God,
My best friend's heart is breaking. What shall I tell her? ~Deb
God ~ Tell her to let not her heart be troubled, and to believe in Me And My son.

Dear God,
My best friend is finding it hard to trust those she once loved. What shall I tell her? ~Deb
God ~ Tell her to Trust in Me and do good.

Dear God,
My best friend needs her joy restored. What shall I tell her? ~Deb
God ~ Tell her, to delight herself in me and I will give her the desires of her heart. Tell her I will restore the joy of her salvation.

Dear God,
My best friend may feel at times that her faith is wavering by what she sees. What shall I tell her? ~Deb
God ~ Tell her, the just shall live by faith. Let her know faith is the substance of things hoped for and the evidence of things not seen. Also, bring to her remembrance "we walk by faith and not by sight".

Continued...

Dear God,
What should my best friend do as she goes before you in prayer? ~ Deb
God ~ be joyous always; pray without ceasing. Know that the fervent effectual prayers of the righteous availeth much.

Dear God,
I miss my best friend from sitting beside me in church as we lift up praises to you. What shall I tell her? ~ Deb
God ~ Tell her, not to forsake assembling herself with others even more so as the day approaches.

Dear Deb,
I've told you what I'm going to do. Now, what are you going to do for your best friend? ~ God

Dear God,
I'm going to send her this letter and let her know, even though she's going through, she can depend on each and every word that you've spoken.
I'm going to remind her, you are her strength and hope and in you, she can find peace. The Peace which surpasses all understanding.
I'm going to let her know when she's finished talking with you, I'll be next in line.
I will let her know I love her and her family and as she goes to you in prayer, I'll also be praying with her. ~ Deb

A Slice of Bacon, Is It Worth It?

During the beginning of each New Year, many people make Resolutions, Promises or whatever name we choose to use for our new Life-changing goals. Well, I'm no different.

During the 1st forty days of the year, my exercise class usually Participates In a forty-day cleansing and fast. Each day we eliminate a particular type of food, including starches, sweets, and carbonated drinks from our daily eating routine. However, for the entire 40 days, we are asked to eliminate meat from our diets completely.

So after 5 days of not eating meat, I thought if I just put 1 slice of bacon in a scrambled egg, I would be able to taste the bacon in every bite. After all, it's just 1 slice, it's not like I'm cheating during my fast or anything like that and besides no one will see me.

You know what? Biting into that one slice of bacon thinking no one will see Me is no different than taking one sip of beer, taking one puff of a cigarette or reading or watching something I shouldn't because I think no one will see me, This will not work.

You know what? Whether it's a slice of bacon during a meatless fast or judging my neighbor, in God's sight, sin is sin. So, I must go back and ask God to forgive me for eating even that one slice of bacon and to remember that someone is Always Watching.

Are We Ever Satisfied? Every Day Can't Be Friday

It's Monday again. As I walk through the doors, I say good morning to her, she always says "good morning sweetie". They greet me with a good morning as I begin to scan my card, good morning back to them as well. Two good mornings, oh it's going to be a good day. We gather at the elevator, sometimes one or two, sometimes three, four or five, yes we're ready to start the day! Should I say good morning? Some have smiles on their faces...some have frowns...should I say good morning? Yes!

How was your weekend to some I ask: (too quick, not long enough, it's over already) are some of the replies. Well, every day can't be Friday.

As the day progresses I meet some in the hallway many I know, some I don't... hello, I say, how are you? Its Monday again some may reply. Ugh, I hate Mondays... Well, every day can't be Friday.

Wow, it's Tuesday already, how are you doing today? The only good thing I say about today is that I'm glad it's not Monday.
Well, every day can't be Friday.

And when did Wednesday get a name change? Are you doing ok today? Yep, its Hump day...is the reply. I wish this week would be over so I can enjoy the weekend. But every day can't be Friday.

And when did Thursday get out of the picture? Now it's just known as Friday Eve. I wish this week would be over so I can enjoy the weekend.

Many times my thoughts and a lot of times my response is, why are we rushing today to get to tomorrow? Why not be thankful today so hopefully, we can have a tomorrow? Each day holds the same amount of hours, minutes and seconds. It's just a different name that's listed on that day.

All I know is, you can always depend on time. Because it will be the same time today as it was yesterday and as it will be tomorrow. So, if we enjoy each and every day, when the weekend comes it should make us more grateful. So, don't Rush it, Friday will come soon enough. Friday is finally here! Now, what???

That's What You Get For Being Late on 1ˢᵗ Sunday

Even though I prayed the prayer for time
And against procrastination on Saturday night,
I still did not prepare my garment for today
Which is 1ˢᵗ Sunday, Communion Service.

I still stayed in the bed longer than I should have;
I left the house at 8:00 am for church when I knew
I should have been sitting in my seat
Ready to usher in the Spirit of the Lord.

So guess what happened when I arrived at church,
I had to sit on the last seat in the back row
Of the church on Communion Sunday.
When it was time to walk with my sisters
To the Communion table, I had to run to get in the line.

It was another 1ˢᵗ Sunday Communion Service
And yes I was late again and dressed in white.
But as I came in the door, an usher met me and asked me to sit upfront
On the 2ⁿᵈ row next to the mothers. Who me…? No…I'm late.
I can't walk in front of all of those people and it's embarrassing.
No, I can't, no I won't, no, no, no.

Now come on Deacon Wife, dressed in white ready to walk
With your sisters to carry the Communion trays
But you can't Obey the Request of the Doorkeeper and
You want to Drink of My Blood and Eat of My Body?

Lord, I'm sorry, I'll sit up front
And next 1ˢᵗ Sunday I'll be on time.

Where Does My Passion, Lie?

Do I have passion, excitement, and enthusiasm for this ministry? Was I called to this ministry or was it thrust upon me because of the duty appointed to my husband? Am I faithful, committed and determined to make a difference?

Do I pray as I should, do I read and study my bible daily? Do I faithfully attend the meetings when they are scheduled or send an email or a call or a call or a call or a call about them or do I let someone know if I'm not able to make it?

Do I call, send a card or make a visit when I hear that one of my fellow sisters or brothers in the ministry is sick or has lost a loved one? Do I send an encouraging word just to let someone know I was thinking about them today?

Does my husband know that I pray for him? Does my daughter see me being kind and showing respect to him? Does she see me honoring my husband as being head of the household?

Do I thank my husband for being a good provider for his family? Do I tell my husband, thank you for coming home to us each night or that I appreciate him for letting us know where he is if he's going to be late?

Do we say good morning to each other when we wake up and goodnight before we go to bed?

In all, we must remember that marriage is a commitment we not only made to each other but foremost to God. So, when we have a strong passion for God, our passion and desire should overflow into our work, our ministry and the Love we have for our spouses.

A Covering

Did you know that God provides a covering for us?

This summer we stayed at a cabin in the mountains of Tennessee. As I sat on the porch of the cabin I realized how beautiful the view was. As I continued sitting, I looked at the design, the Builders used to construct this cabin. I noticed the big pieces of grand oak wood both inside and out.

One morning as we began to eat breakfast one of our friends asked did I hear the rain, the thunder and did I see the lightning flashing last night? Even though it rained hard last night, thunder and lightning came but today the porch is only a little damp. Lightning and rain I said, what time was this?

As they described the occurrences of the night I realized I did not hear a thing. All I could hear was the soft remnants of a rain shower. This reminded me that even when trouble and crisis surround us God can keep us in perfect peace through it all. Yes, I hurt but, yes sickness came upon me but, yes finances were hard but, God Covered Me.

Complete

You fought a good fight, you kept the faith
You've finished your course; you've won your race.
Your race to victory that you strived for each day
Asking God to lead, protect and guide you every step of the way.

I know that Jesus is the first face you want to see, but second, in line will be
your Bride Mary for whom you longed to be with.
Now together in glory, you can both rejoice,
Because a long time ago you made Jesus your choice.

The same choice you presented to us your children, each and everyone,
from the oldest to the youngest and the newest one just born.
The life you lived dad means so much to me
because you set godly examples and you've left your legacy.
The legacy you showed for each of us to follow,
day by day and even into tomorrow.

Although your body became very weak,
your mind and your faith always remained strong.
Yes, strong enough to praise us when we did right
-and strong enough to chastise when we did wrong.

A wonderful father you've always been,
from the very beginning and even to the end.
Yes, we'll miss you each and every day,
but we're thankful that you've taught us how to love,
forgive and how to pray.

You told us this day would surely come; but yet it's still hard to believe,
though our hearts are aching yes we are sad, but Oh what a joy in knowing
that Your Soul is Now rejoicing-because God has made you Glad!

It is now, Complete!

In Memory of Deacon William Hayes Sr.

Baby Girl

Sometimes I can't put into words the things I want to say to you;
But this one thing I do know, you've got to see it through.
You're so close to the finish line just a few more miles to go;
So please don't walk away right now, just breathe and take it slow:

Once you get that 2nd wind, your strength will be renewed
Then your pace will pick up again, to do what you need to do
So just remember I'm cheering for you
As you get closer to your finished goal:
Then you'll look back and say thank you Lord for going through
This trial, because you've strengthened my soul.

So if you need to cry and release let this be the day,
Take your time off for lunch and go home so you can pray;
I'm sure God will tell you what He wants you to do,
As you pray for strength and grace to see this last week through!

**BE ENCOURAGED MY FRIEND, JUST A LITTLE TIME MORE,
JUST REMEMBER, YOU'LL BE LEAVING THIS WINDOW AND
HEADING THROUGH ANOTHER DOOR.**

I USED THE DISHWASHER TODAY

I was in the kitchen one day washing the dishes. I think I'm always in the kitchen washing dishes. Yes, complaining, as usual, how come I always end up in the kitchen, why do I always have to be the one to wash the dishes, "actually he washes them as much as I do if not more". Every time I turn around I'm always in the kitchen. Dishes, Dishes, Dishes, didn't I just wash these dishes an hour ago? Who put this plate down here when I wasn't looking and where did this fork come from? Then I look to the right of me, and there I saw it, a big black shiny machine and written on it in big bold letters were the words GE Profile.

I looked at it some more and found that this machine had buttons with numbers, pictures and many settings on it. I was curious so I decided to open it up, to my surprise; this machine had baskets that could fit plates, forks, knives, even pots, and pans. Then I asked myself a few questions: why did this machine still have tape around it? Why did it still have a small unopened bottle of Cascade still wrapped up? Could this machine be a dishwasher? Has it been here the entire 5 years we've been living in this house?

Well for the next set of dishes to be cleaned I had an idea, I will use the dishwasher. So I put the plates, the forks and knives, the pots and the pans all in their places. I poured the dishwashing liquid and pushed those magic buttons and wow! I used the dishwasher today!

Note Sometimes if we just look around we may realize that we've already been provided with the tools we need to get the job done.

Everything You Need, God's got it!

I tried to find love in the arms of a man, but that didn't do it, God's got it.
I tried to find peace from a bottle and a can, but that didn't do it, God's got it.
I tried to get high by smoking on some weed, but that didn't do it,
God's got it.
I tried to get through by planting a big seed, but that didn't do it, God's got it.
I hid behind a smile and tried to hide my pain, but that didn't do it,
God's got it.
The smile only lasted for just a little while, nothing from it I gained.
I thought I'd be healed through a doctor and some pills ~ but that didn't do it,
God's got it.
Had to learn for myself that God is the only one who can heal because I know
God's got it.
Tried to find joy in temporary things, but that didn't do it,
God's got it.
Like houses, land and money and even some bling, bling, but that didn't do it,
God's got it.

So…

The man ran out, peace subsided, the high came down,
Seeds didn't grow, the pain returned, the smile wore off, pills didn't heal,
The house was recalled, the money disappeared.

Then…

My spirit got low and the faith I had left was just a tiny little bit.
But it made me realize everything I need,
My God, He's already got it!

I Saw a Little Bird Sitting on a Tree

I saw a little bird sitting on a tree,
He said Good Morning, Deborah as he looked back at me.

I said hi little red bird what are you doing up there?
He said I'm doing my daily meditations, now did you say your prayers?

Yes, little red bird, I did say my prayers,
Then God told me to see what's happening out here.

I'm the little red bird doing what I do,
Sitting on the tree limb looking in on you.

I saw that your heart was aching,
That you had lost your smile,
Things hadn't been going well for you, for now, a little while.

Start smiling again the little bird begins to say,
It may be hard right now but tomorrow is another day.

I Give You My Permission

Hi Ladies,
I just want to let you know, I give you my permission to share my Lover.

I give you my permission to call on Him anytime during the day, or night.
I give you my permission to call Him Big Daddy.
I give you my permission to ask Him to supply all of your needs.
I give you my permission to ask Him to help you pay your bills.
I give you my permission to ask Him to be your lover when you're lonely at night.
I give you my permission to have Him be the father of your children.
I give you my permission to take Him with you to work, home and even on vacation.
I give you my permission to ask Him to provide you with shelter.
I give you my permission to Honor and Worship Him.
I give you my permission to ask Him to heal your body when you're not feeling well.
I give you my permission to have Him comfort you when a loved one leaves you in death.
I give you my permission to ask My Lover to be your all and all.

And Gentlemen,
You can share my Lover too. Not only is He Good for the Ladies, But He is also Good for you too.

Still Alive

Often times I feel my face, and yes it's still warm.

That's when I remember,
I am only flesh and soon this body will turn cold,
Into dust and return back to the ground from which it was formed.

That's when I remember,
God, the Father issued us this flesh as only a holding place
For our spirit and someday only the spirit will remain.

Again, I feel my face and yet it's still warm.
Thank You, Lord, for another chance.

What a Week!

Monday ~
Someone called the house to say one of our family members
Had passed away during the night.

Tuesday ~
A friend told us her young daughter tried to commit suicide;

Wednesday ~
A friend called and said her cancer has spread from her colon
To her stomach, her lungs and now in her back.
Hospice has been called in because there's nothing more
Doctors can do. The money's running low and the bills have to be
paid. During this time, my pastor was teaching on Miracles.
I encouraged her to stick out her hand because there was
'Something still in the Barrel'.

Even in her sickness, she asked me 'hey girl, what've you been up
too?' How are your daughter and husband? Some nerve she has.
Oh yeah, she asked, 'And how are John and his wife Mary doing?
When you see them tell then I said hello and I'm praying for them'.

Thursday ~
I got to work and found out a friends' relative has been raped by
her Stepfather, one week away from her high school graduation.
Oh, did I mention, he was a pastor at a church in the area?

Friday ~
When I got to work my team leader came to say goodbye.
No explanation, no reasoning!
He was gone.

Salt

The word salt to me means flavor, seasoning or leavening.
As with any seasoning, if too much is added to the dish or the pot, what's inside loses its appeal and sometimes the taste is so strong and overpowering you may not be able to eat that which has been prepared.
Sometimes you may have to water it down and even discard what already
Has been prepared because too much seasoning can be overbearing.

The Bible states us as Christians are the salt of the earth; us, meaning those who have been washed in the blood, while we are on the earth, we can be the ones who add flavor to the bland things that have no life. We are the ones who are to encourage those who are low, despondent or who have not yet accepted Jesus as their Lord and Savior.

Even though we may be the salt, we must still be careful how we
Approach those who are hurting and how we distribute that which God has placed in us.

As with natural salt, if we as God's disciples' come on too strong to those we are witnessing to, sometimes we can lead them astray or turn them away from Him, whom we are trying to get them closer to.

We as witnesses are to add to or approach those we are trying to reach little by little just enough to give them a hint of how good our God is and how good He can be to them. Once they receive a little taste, we want to make them hunger for more; we don't want to overwhelm them.
Remember too much salt all at one time is not always good;
for it can cause you high blood pressure.

We have to be salt by our actions, our talk, how we respond to others,
How we visit the sick or offer a prayer for those who are in need.
We have to share a testimony with them,
Because I'm sure we each have more than one.

So remember, when making God's word come to life sometimes we have to
Share a little, at a time and after a while, you'll see those who you witnessed to, Begin to check the recipe book (Bible) for themselves.
That's when you know that your salt has been applied
With the right amount of measurements.

Committed?

A friend just asked me to read something she wrote about one of the Ministries she is involved with at her church. There she works with students both girls and boys who are currently or will be in the 6th and 7th grades. Her topic was what kind of bridge she sees herself as while she teaches impressionable children.

Is she a bridge in a deck of cards that if they fall they will scatter? Is she a bridge that if torn down no one will notice? No, she sees herself as God sees her, glowing with strength for these youth to travel across and gain knowledge of where they've been and for them to look to see what good things lie ahead. As she wrote about being a teacher to these students, she stated a teacher should have passion, determination, commitment, and faithfulness.

Actually, before she came to my desk I was just contemplating my passion for the ministry in which I teach the children. Do I have passion? Was I called to do it or was it just a volunteer activity to give something back to those who teach my daughter every Sunday morning and every Tuesday night?

Yet, I ask myself where my passion lies within the ministry. Even though I am a part of many, am I faithful and committed to any? Because just showing up at meetings do not always show commitment but am I determined to make a difference in any of them?

Do I pray as I should, do I both read and study my bible on a daily basis? Do I encourage others when they are going through (passion)? Do I faithfully attend meetings or if I'm not able to make it do I let someone know (commitment)?

Does my 10-year-old daughter see or hear me rightly dividing the word of truth?

I am often in awe of my husband as I see him studying and asking questions about the scriptures. Does he ever see me praying, does he see me studying?

If not, why not start today.

A Note about the Author

I was born in Columbia, SC in a community called Arthurtown, not many miles from where I currently reside. Growing up in this close-knit community taught me the value of love, honesty, and respect.

*M*y husband, William, and I have been married for 38 years. With our daughter Danielle now in college and our son Cedric married with 3 children of his own, we are now empty nesters.

*Thank You for reading my poetry.
It's inspired me over the years.
I hope you find Peace and Encouragement
Somewhere in these pages that are pieces of me,
To help you make it through, Right Now!*